GUFF

Brendan Kennelly's Guff is both mouthpiece and mouthed-off, Devil's advocate and self critic, everyman and every writer consumed by self-doubt and self-questioning. The book of Guff is about words writing the man. Words drive him into the cave of himself where he questions everything including words that seem to constitute answers and answers that question both questions and answers.

Do poets write poems or do poems write poets? And consider the shape of that question-mark, like a snake twisting in its sleep: so twisting, or twisted snakes, lie beside Guff as he tries to sleep in his cave, led now by the words that the snake hisses in his old head. All through his book-length poem Guff hears both the hissing of the words he believes he loves as well as the hissing mysteries of love. Guff is prey to the ruthless continuity of one word leading to another, until these words relax and settle down into what he thinks, or hopes, is *meaning*.

Like Kennelly's *Cromwell*, *The Book of Judas* and *Poetry My Arse*, Guff is a knockabout Swiftian satire, a mischievous meditation on the human condition. It's also a powerfully expressive hymn to life with all its flaws, a snaking poem with the movement of a river in its different moods from cold anger to summer warmth for minds and bodies, which asks who or what is a genuinely noble person? Dublin is the backdrop to Guff's jabbering quest, a city where haunted men walk the streets talking to themselves, at times with passion, at times with an air of secrecy or self-accusation, at times as if seeking a friend prepared to listen. Guff is a brother to these strange wanderers. In the poem he becomes at one or at odds with them.

Brendan Kennelly was born in 1936 in Ballylongford, Co. Kerry, and was Professor of Modern Literature at Trinity College, Dublin from 1973 until his retirement in 2005. He has published more than 30 books of poetry, including *Familiar Strangers: New & Selected Poems 1960-2004* (2004), which includes the whole of his book-length poem *The Man Made of Rain* (1998). He is best-known for two controversial poetry books, *Cromwell*, published in Ireland in 1983 and in Britain by Bloodaxe in 1987, and his epic poem *The Book of Judas* (1991), which topped the Irish bestsellers list: a shorter version was published by Bloodaxe in 2002 as *The Little Book of Judas*. His third epic, *Poetry My Arse* (1995), did much to outdo these in notoriety. All these remain available separately from Bloodaxe, along with his more recent titles: *Glimpses* (2001), *Martial Art* (2003), *Now* (2006), *Reservoir Voices* (2009), *The Essential Brendan Kennelly: Selected Poems*, edited by Terence Brown and Michael Longley, with audio CD (2011), and *Guff* (2013).

His drama titles include *When Then Is Now* (2006), a trilogy of his modern versions of three Greek tragedies (all previously published by Bloodaxe): Sophocles' *Antigone* and Euripides' *Medea* and *The Trojan Women*. His *Antigone* and *The Trojan Women* were both first performed at the Peacock Theatre, Dublin, in 1986 and 1993 respectively; *Medea* premièred in the Dublin Theatre Festival in 1988, toured in England in 1989 and was broadcast by BBC Radio 3. His other plays include Lorca's *Blood Wedding* (Northern Stage, Newcastle & Bloodaxe, 1996).

His translations of Irish poetry are available in *Love of Ireland: Poems from the Irish* (Mercier Press, 1989). He has edited several anthologies, including *The Penguin Book of Irish Verse* (1970/1981), *Ireland's Women: Writings Past and Present*, with Katie Donovan and A. Norman Jeffares (Gill & Macmillan, 1994), and *Dublines*, with Katie Donovan (Bloodaxe Books, 1995), and published two early novels, *The Crooked Cross* (1963) and *The Florentines* (1967).

His *Journey into Joy: Selected Prose*, edited by Åke Persson, was published by Bloodaxe in 1994, along with *Dark Fathers into Light*, a critical anthology on his work edited by Richard Pine. John McDonagh's critical study *Brendan Kennelly: A Host of Ghosts* was published in The Liffey Press's Contemporary Irish Writers series in 2004.

BRENDAN KENNELLY

GUFF

A poem

BLOODAXE BOOKS

ISBN: 978 1 85224 983 0

First published 2013 by
Bloodaxe Books Ltd,
Highgreen,
Tarset,
Northumberland NE48 1RP.

www.bloodaxebooks.com
For further information about Bloodaxe titles
please visit our website or write to
the above address for a catalogue.

Supported by
**ARTS COUNCIL
ENGLAND**

ACKNOWLEDGEMENT

Some of these poems were featured on *Work in Progress*
on BBC Radio 3 in 2001.

Cover design: Neil Astley & Pamela Robertson-Pearce.

Printed in Great Britain by Bell & Bain Limited, Glasgow, Scotland, on
acid-free paper sourced from mills with FSC chain of custody certification.

MIX
Paper from
responsible sources
FSC
www.fsc.org   FSC® C007785

GUFF

GUFF

Speech

Guff gave a speech on behalf of the deaf
        and dumb of Ireland.
Am I, he asked himself as he speeched, really
        guilty of this almost torrential shite?
I am, he answered, to thunderous applause.
        Slept with a deaf and dumb beauty that night.
He could have sworn she gigglemocked
        in morning light.

Take care

Take care of words, the old voice said.
Take loving care of words.

Guff heard.

Does he take care of words?

Guff is Guff.

'Nuff said.

He'd talk the leg off a skillet,
persuade a gun to donate a bullet
to a worthy cause.

Guff knows all the laws.

Words serve him.
He does not serve words.

Mouth.

Prison of Joy

Guff teaches Psychology and Law
in the Prison of Joy.

The prisoners love him.
He talks law, he talks psychology,
they don't talk back.

One prisoner said to Guff, You're good.
Thank you. I want to show my appreciation.
May I do a knee-cappin' job for you?

Not now, Guff said, not now.
Who knows? Later, maybe.

The prisoner retired to his sentence.

Guff got the bus back to town,
saw many people
talking to themselves.

Nobody would ever know
about
what.

Nobody can be sentenced for that.

About

That night, Guff talked about
    Lamb chops
    The sinking of the Titanic
    The Battle of the Somme
    The Holocaust
    DNA
    Leisure Centres
    Hiroshima
    Smoking and criminality
    The first heart transplant
    The Revised Leaving Certificate English Syllabus
    Miscarriages
    Aspects of Modern Verse
    The nature of the Curse

Then Guff shut up
    apart from a few revelations
    about Jews, Arabs and Muslims.

He went to bed
    fell asleep
    dreamed of talking
    with Tom Mix, Roy Rogers
    Gene Autrey, John Wayne,
    Hopalong Cassidy, Gabby Hayes
    and the Cisco Kid.

O the things they told him
about heroes, outlaws, money, blood!

It's a pity he had to wake up
but wake up he did
coffeeed, radioed,

Two murders in Limerick
one murder in Dublin

farmers on strike
nurses on strike
60 extra cars in Dublin and the New Year
is only a month old

he drank more coffee,
swallowed more words
flying like hungry birds through his brain

He washed, dressed, went for a walk
in the chattering Dublin rain.

When Guff gets going
there's nothing he can't explain.
Once every few years, he wonders why,
goes for a walk in the rain.
Explainers, he says, should sometimes be pissed on.
It gets Guff going all over again.

Post-Christmas cough

Guff spoofed.
It was all about the paradoxical gravelly
      beauty of her post-Christmas cough.
She yawned, considered.
Took her clothes off.

The Guff principle

Guff saw Descartes in Asdee.
Thinking.

Guff saw Tarzan up a tree.
Guff put two and two together.
Nothing.

Guff swapped addition for blazing heather.
Sparkling.

That which bores is bad.
That which animates is good.
(Guff loves making proverbs of his own).

Without further ado
he set fire to his mind
in a way that will not be mentioned here

lest it stimulates others to imitate
the Guff Principle
which Tarzan and Descartes avoid
because they
have their own way

of seeing things
and doing things,

their own way

which, as far as Guff can see,
works well enough for them

on terra firma
or up a tree.

meetings

Guff went to fourteen meetings in three days.

On the evening of the third day
he sat in his cave and ate a mixture
of Weetabix   Special K   Shredded Wheat Bitesize
Linusit Gold   All-Bran Plus Naturally low in Fat
and Original Muesli Country Store.

He ate it all, as if taking revenge.
Then he ate some more.

Then he drank a bottle of Jameson

and thanked God
that out of the fourteen meetings
assiduously attended
he couldn't remember
a single fucking sentence.

Guff silently
breathed thanks to heaven
for the crucial advantages
of a defective memory.

Forgetfulness is the key to a happy eternity.

Hanging on

Guff approached her, her hair
was dyed a furious Celtic red.
'You are transformed,' he ventured.
'Kiss my clit,' she said.

He did not.
He determined instead
to immerse himself
in ancient Celtic myth
convinced
that the most effective way
to understand
this woman of the New Age
was to sniff the mythical origins
of Maeve's and Deirdre's rage.

He read and read and read.
One night, in bed with Deirdre,
he asked her what he considered
an original question.
        She saw red.
'Kiss my clit,' she said.
He did.
Her clit went to his head.
He nearly died

but he hung on, hung on
as only the gruff Guff can,

a sticky, gobby, flower-o'-the flock man
you might meet on a Wicklow hill
                or down a Dublin lane.

All the mythic tales slipped out the window
and turned to magic mushrooms in a meadow.

Second Line

A heroic couplet danced in Guff's head
but the second line sniggered, scooted off.

Guff searched high and low and far and wide
like a fraught stressed bridegroom who has lost his bride.

The lady's vanished, sir, the west wind sighed.
To this day, Guff can't tell if the west wind lied.

Sad

Guff was sad.
He walked barefoot in the rain.
He passed another broken castle
patient in the wind.
He thought it was Buddha
squatting among the rocks.
He picked his way among jellyfish,
they had a bad name
like taxdodgers with money in foreign accounts.
Guff took trouble not to count them.
He saw a brown stone a white stone
among infinite greyblack gravel.
Rain hammered his head.
The left side of his head was ice.
He found a golfball, he knew
everything on earth may be nothing.
He heard the sea coughing, was it sick?
The left side of his head could have sunk the Titanic.
Grass wagged like gossipy tongues.

Guff listened.
He heard a few squeaks and cries.
The sun came through like a bit of news
to refresh the heart and brighten the mind.
Then the sun took the boat to England
Guff looked at a name in the sand.
T O M.
There was a face in the O.
It smiled.
Not for long.
Vanished with the flick of a wave.
Guff saw a sparrow up and down
and over and back like a bit of favourite Mozart.
Guff's hands were turning blue.
Wind and rain have the knack.
Guff thought of that one drunken night in Stalingrad.
Barefoot, freezing, he was home.
Sad, but not too sad.
Too sad is when words are so useless
they are fire made of snow
burning in a legend centuries ago.

Knowledge

Her buttocks know they're being evaluated.
Eyes shift to the West Coast.
Her buttocks know the history and geography of eyes, updated.
Guff does not. One more way of being lost.

Trying

'You should change your life drastically
at least once every ten years,'
she whispered quietly
to Guff.

'Change? But what is there to change?'
he asked.

'You mean you don't know
what you would like to change?'

'No.'

'Well, then, stay as you are, dear Guff,' she smiled.
'Scratch your head, live with your shadows,
Try to dream
of the randy and the wild.'

'I will,' he promised. 'I'll try to dream.
That's what I like best. trying to dream.
Failing, of course, but trying nonetheless.
If I could truly dream, would I know success?'

Old fashioned

Wandering through himself Guff knows he's old fashioned.
He wears a waistcoat.
He opens doors for women.
He spits deep in his hankie
and stuffs it quickly back in his pocket.
He wears shirt and tie on a beach.

He likes poems that rhyme
and will not condone
a shapeless freeverse moan.
He writes long letters
and likes to receive long letters.
He feels guilty masturbating.
The Christian Brothers said
the hair would fall off his head
and grow out of the palms of his hands instead.
He has no wish to be known as
     Hairyhands Guff the Wanker.
He's a moral being, he is, he truly believes
     he is, but not always.
He likes a bath on a Saturday night,
     and Confession once a month.
He doesn't like words like fuck or cunt
and cannot understand why they appear
in state-of-the-art dictionaries.
He doesn't know what art is, anyway,
and doesn't trust people who say they do.
Yet he has a nose for the good, the beautiful, the true.
He gave up running forty years ago
and likes to walk
in a lazy stately manner
down sidestreets and laneways
of graffiti-spattered Dublin.
He salutes only those he knows,
with a certain reticence.
He would not call himself Victorian
but likes moral maxims
and ladies in long dresses.
Sometimes he feels mad
and carries a red screwdriver in his pocket
purely for safety's sake.
You never know, do you?
Some nutter could jump on you
from a doorway in Empress Lane
and, then, well, it's you or him.
Guff is a fifty-fifty man.

Not born yet

Be yourself, says he, you're at home anywhere.
Hope, says he, is the physician of all misery.
My mind, says he, is the only property law cannot seize.
Guff mutters such words when he strolls through himself
as though he were a strange old city
some lunatic may bomb at any moment
but a young woman, not born yet,
will restore to its former elegance
out of love and admiration.
Not born yet. Her parentlovers haven't even met.
But meet they will, and time will turn
to face the music when that girl is born.

Realm of gold

Guff writes in his notebook:
            Ireland's greatest achievement
            is that it survived the Irish.

These words have the smell of truth,
            he says to the notebook.

The notebook says nothing, just
                        hoards the words
            like the secret rich
                        their spondoolicks.

The rich build a wall around their lives
            where they tend their secrets
like specially imported flowers.
            The flowers call the shots.

The words of the rich should be listened to.
Do you know what style is? Guff asks his notebook.
The notebook knows what questions not to answer
like many a successful dealer.

Answering questions is a picky art.
  It can turn you
into a dancer or a diplomat
    with a multiple point of view.

It can make you long for a rude,
    outspoken spitty fucker
who shoves stylish souls into silence
    with his whack of a knacker

before he ups and shags off
    into an outcast mould
that Guff's notebook chronicles
    as a realm of gold.

bells

Guff sat with the rapist on a bench near the Cathedral
and listened to his version of the horror
that began in the Dublin slums.
Cathedral bells began to ring.
All the rapist's teeth had fallen out but
    he went on grinding his gums.

picture

When Guff says 'Be with me now'
　　he looks the picture
　　　　in the eye

(how the centuries fly by)

　　　　and sees the face of one
　　　　　who will not die.

Road

Guff thought of the woman who locked herself into her house
and said what she had to say.
This was valiant and fruitful and yet, Guff had to admit, not
the only way.

He knew a woman who spraddled the loins of midnight
and came into her glory.
Style is the toll on the road chosen by loneliness,
walking with sorrow without feeling sorry.

one line

If I could write one line to praise you sufficiently
for all you've done
and continue to do,
      I would be happy, happy
Guff said to the water

          the water
    cleaning
rock gravel stone
    cleaning
filth of woman and man
    cleaning
the often befouled sand,

    just one line
one, I would be happy, Guff said,

but I can't, I can't,
    not one line
not a single line of praise
    that might justify
my foolish, ruminating days.

bad blood

Guff reads a book of bad blood
The book of bad blood reads Guff
He doesn't like being read by a book
He likes to feel the mastery of reading
The self-inflating power of acquisition and possession
but now, late at night, he's being read
he gets a smell of his own vanity
a whiff of his own pathetic smallness of heart and mind
a sense of his own begrudgery
a cold awareness of his soul's poverty
and he knows
he is, frequently, a notorious bollocks
who doesn't know he's a notorious bollocks.
Guff, slightly breathless, lays the book aside
gives it an ugly look
in return for its gift of revelation.
He sits and ponders through the night.
In the first shy light of dawn
he feels a strange, calm surge of gratitude for the gift.
He murmurs 'Thank you' to the book
and goes to bed
in the company of his own bad blood.

Recovery

Guff is lost in the swirling talk,
a gull's feather in the stormy Shannon.
Guff recovers, talks, talks. She listens.

So now who's your money on?
Gamble if you will. Find the feather if you can.
Guess the depth of the river
between the woman and the man.

If both should venture in,
who will drown?

how

It all comes down
to how the psychologist
interprets available
information on the serial
killer who came into
the world like you or me
then turned to pleasure
of an almost
ungraspable kind
and looked often
at the plump photograph
on his kitchen wall.
Guff listens, listens,
frozen by ice
Fort Knoxing it all.

It is

I'm allergic to dinosaurs, she said.
I'm allergic to cats eating sausages
on window-sills and
I'm allergic to crocodiles trying to do a riverdance.
What are you allergic to? she asked Guff.
        (she was three, this is not
giving the game away)

I'm allergic to myself, he said.
The only thing for you to do, she blitzed,
        is to go on scratching your head.
        Scratching
        is good for your fingers
                your nails
                your hair
                your skin
                your mind
                your soul
                isn't that so?
It is, said Guff.
Thank you, she said. You're not such
a sad old dinosaur, after all.

left of logic

Following a sign unrecognised by law
Guff turned left of logic and saw

      stones dancing on a stage
      of shiny wet sand,
      a feather standing up
      like a year-old determined to walk,
      a broken shell and God
      knows who took the pearl,
      the skeleton
      of a July Christmas tree
      homaging a golf-course,
      rocks remembering Civil War,
      rocks challenging the Atlantic,
      father and son hurling
      in Croke Park sunlight,
            children
      screaming at their first encounter
      with cold water,
      screaming in that country
          left of logic
where Guff walked for awhile
         before he returned
         to his rented cave
and gave himself, for the first time in fifteen years,
         a haircut.
In a state of capital delight
         he slickscissorsed the hair from his head.

Of how many logical lads may this be said?

Hobbling

Guff listens. Family history. She's trying to make sense.

'My dad's a lawyer,' she says.

'My dad's a liar,' she says.

The words hobble each other.

'What's the difference,' she quickens, it is not a question.

'The trouble is,' she slows, 'my dad
        has a language of his own.
The man is his language.
        The language is the man.
Why do his words make my dad such an also-ran?'

rainy day

Guff puts his ear to the wind,
shuts his eyes and listened.
'What's your language?' he asked the wind.
The wind laughed, whistled, rumbled.
'What's your language?' Guff asked again.
The wind called in the rain
and belted Guff on his listening ear.
'There's language for you,' mouthed Guff
scuttling to shelter behind a wall
while he grew thoughtful.
'I suppose I shouldn't be so cheeky
as to ask the wind what its language is
when I'm not so sure of my own.
Suppose the wind put the question to me
what would my answer be?
He couldn't say.
He promised himself that if he ever
stumbled on an accurate answer
he'd save it
for a rainy day.

A letter

Guff writes a letter.
He knows what he wants to say
but doesn't say it.
something is throttling him.
No, not a lie, just an inability
to say what he believes he knows.
He starts again.
The words mock him after two sentences.
They sneer at him, their eyes cruel with ridicule.
They form a jibing chorus,
they say
>   You're a dumb fool
>   You're a back o' the class lad
>   You're a forging eejit,
>   You can't tell a right word
>   from the hawk or a crow
>   and you'll never know
>   that you don't know.

Guff is battered but not beaten.
He hugs his black biro.
He kisses it.
The biro smiles, an old friend,
and blood left in it still,
Guff moves it forward,
it moves Guff forward,
a letter is being written
in a room somewhere

to a person
in a room somewhere.
Guff is taking off, doesn't care
he doesn't know that he doesn't know,
something is being said,
maybe a bit sad or uncouth
or malicious or loving or rough,

but it's there
and it's time to rest the black biro.
I think of you often, how did you feel
when she upped and took the boat?
                    Write sometime,
                              love,
                                        Guff.

he felt he was

He sat and listened to the lecturer
talking about metaphor.

Guff couldn't understand most of it.

Walking the streets afterwards
he felt he was
testicular cancer
a fly in the Ryder Cup
a plastic spoon up to its neck in sand
a blind magpie
a used teabag not fit for a bin

and, as now and then in childhood,

first cousin to a venial sin.

There. There.

I know, murmurs Guff, there are those who work
so that killings may never cease.
There are worse things than the sight of blood.
Anything is better than peace.

The tradition of going to America
        will reward us with guns.
After all, the Irish built Boston,
        Famine's daughters and sons.

Five or six are enough to keep
        the evil flame alive.
If we forget our jigs and reels
        we can always jive.

Consider the Tiger's children,
        their teeth, hair, brains, eyes.
Is there a truth in ignorance?
        Is education lies?

Is freedom money? Money, freedom?
        Ask your man on hunger-strike.
When I retire will they give me a telly
        or a deadly motorbike?

Today, Guff is afraid of answers
        but the questions won't stop.
Why can't I settle, he asks himself,
        for a chatty corner-shop?

Why can't I join a Party
        and work for a decent end?
Do I know the meaning of enemy?
        The value of friend?

Do I even know what I think,
        when a man of twenty-three
is found battered to death on waste ground
        or hanging from a tree?

And the talkers on telly and radio,
        do they know what they say?
Are all the words they pick and give
        helplessly blown away

like dust on the wind, dust on the wind
        that might blind you a while
if you didn't know how to cope with dust
        hamstringing your style?

Guff goes to the door of his cave.
        In the city he hears the sea.
He notes the bond between clouds and waves.
        He never heard of me.

Why should he, in the name of all
        jiving 'twixt peace and war
bother his head with man or beast,
        with spud or star?

Guff stands at the door, looks out and up
        and down and here and there.
What does it mean to kill? he asks.
        what does it mean to care?

Guffprayer

Jesus of the cold ocean
    the dangerous caves
        the screaming children
            the broken glass in the sand
please sweep through my sleep tonight.

Am I a living witness
    or a smelly mouthful of air?
Why is daylight a curse for some?
    For others, a kind of prayer?

Head down, Guff closes the door,
    sits in his patient chair.
The nighthours slowly shuffle past.
    When day comes, Guff is there.

There. There. Guff is there. Silent. Thoughful eyes
    staring, as before,
at the street that has no answers
    but the traffic's morning roar

late

In the long meadow, the blackbird
    sings heavenwards for its mate.
Why should heaven trouble to listen
    when the echo is always late?

Tides

The tide is out
    the tide is in
Guff is happy
    as he's ever been

The tide is in
    the tide is out
Guff's heart grows
    dark with doubt

Who's that lying
    face down in the sand
a clutch of seaweed
    in either hand?

The people look
    and walk away
Guff looks and heads
    towards Aoife Quilty

who danced the time
    of the sun's eclipse
a seasmile dancing
    on her lips

What does it mean
    never to rest?
The moon has its laws
    the earth is crossed

and Aoife Quilty
    will not move
till a fist of seaweed
    promises love

Work and fun

Guff works with the rhythms.
'It's fun,' one rhythm says, 'living
beyond your reach, letting you near,
        child learning to walk,
                possessing you.'

Guff works with the rhythms, hoping they're true.
The rhythms play with old Guff,
        it's what they love to do.
How did you get to heaven? Flew.

Corners

Guff likes to talk to himself, to others.
It all may be nothing.
Yet dialogue is a wondrous thing.

A small island
in one corner of which
people kill
each other –
is that where you come from? she asked Guff.

It is, he replied.

And where in that small island
do you live? she asked.

In a corner, he smiled. Of my mind.
A small island compels you to live in your head.
That's why we kill each other, he said.
Poems bloom out of butchered blood.

Are there many corners in the island? she asked.

As many as are in my mind.

Do you know them all?

No, he said, no. Only a few.

So you'll never know the full picture?

True, he said. True.

Why, then, do you scour the small corners of your island mind?

To find the little I can find.

You're a hunter of small shadows, Guff, she said.

Guff said nothing. Scratched his head.
He loves a good ould scratch. What can you say to
a scratcher who sniffs his way through the dialogues of Plato?

Smells

Guff didn't wash for a month
yet he guffed Lettie Pryce into bed.
'You smell like fresh roses,' he murmured.

'You smell like a whore's handbag,' she said.

'If lies were truth, you'd be a sweet-scented bitch.'
'And if shite was cash, Guff, you'd be rich.'

hard to know

It's hard to know, talking to some women,
        whether I'm right or wrong, Guff said
            to an old friend

who nodded and said

Twenty years ago I chose
to walk a straight road
rather than go round a bend.

Guff went foetal in a corner of his mind.
It made no difference in the end.

A whole weekend

Guff went on retreat,
said nothing for a whole weekend
although the words ran up and down his blood
exploded in his mind
like small bombs
some patriotic lunatic
hurls at a coffee-shop.

Imagine that!
A whole weekend without uttering a word!
On the bus back to his cave
Guff sat in a back seat, alone,
sang a song
with fifty-seven verses
which included
statements of love and hate
living and dying
and a soul-touching harvest
of blessings and curses.

noble

Words float swim sink drown in Guff
tonight it's noble
what is a noble thing person place?
     He went to Reading
love murder gaol shame (he had his train fare)
     by all let this be heard
Guff spends days examining manuscripts
     noble
     no bell
     Noble
if the word is lost is the feeling extinct?
     are there graveyards for words?
     who goes to their funeral?
     where is noble buried?
who pauses to say a prayer?

     by all let this be heard
     think of the laughing givers
     at the funeral of a word

Guff goes on his knees
     when a knowing happens
his head slips to his chest
     that word did its best

     now it's gone to its eternal rest

     maybe Guff will write a song about it
     and when he rises from his knees
     sing the song

for noble noble noble
     that suffered wrong

Teeshirt

On Guff's teeshirts are depicted musical instruments
       once banned in Iran
including the home-made fiddle,
       heaving melodeon,
flute, tin whistle, bodhran made of goatskin
Guff wonders when Iran
will play in Dunsink and Bundoran.

He'll get a new teeshirt then,
wear it under his waistcoat,
the envy of unmusical men.

When words melt in music's arms
Guff's teeshirt is a cloak of charms.

It must be added, though, that Guff
never strays far from words
which are his way of seeing
and saying what is and what is not
This, as Mozart once suggested,
is quite a lot.

notes

Adventurous rain plays crucifying notes
       on Guff's open nerves.
Each man gets the Christ
       he deserves.

a strange cruelty

Why does he laugh when Guff
tells him of the young woman's pain?
It is a strange cruelty, difficult
to measure, impossible to explain.
He's a decent man.

Guff knows it has something to do with pleasure
of a remote, entangled kind
like barbed wire caging a woman
watched by a man with a serious mind

capable of devoting years of his life
to the study of, for example, How sick is Shakespeare?
Tonight, someone will rip a young woman apart.
a serious mind will define the darkness of art
Guff will hear laughter mocking his stupid heart.

Swallow

Guff found a dead swallow in Dame Street,
a packed litter-bin its grave.
He said, 'What could I not have made of you,
if I had found you still alive?'

Guff saw the swallow in its own sky,
        its flight accurate and wild
predicting before it earthed to die,
        the birth of a wonder-child.

before he became

Nobody owns Guff (he believes).
He has no wish (he is convinced) to own another.
Possession is a killer of love, the tinker said
        before he became a traveller

and began to wonder who was his brother,

learning all the profitable tricks,
importing drugs to Kinnegad
        smuggling petrol over the Border

never paying a penny tax.

Neighbour

Next door to Guff a terrorist is settling down
to what is known as freedom
after seventeen years in prison.

(Didn't serve the full term, they rarely do.)
He's an easygoing man, watchful
for what may come out of the blue.

He's had enough of what
he once did with terrifying skill:
kill.

He's a quiet neighbour. Love thy neighbour
as thyself. Does Guff love himself?
How may he know?
He sees his neighbour come and go

through light and dark, in sun and rain.
Come. Go. Leave. Stay. Freedom.
Do the dead know pain?
Is it only in silence that the dead
        may live again?

A truly peaceful spot

In the Isle of Innisfree
a 22-apartment development
is being planned
by Pre-Raphaelite Properties.
Underground car parking
is a happy fact.
This is a truly peaceful spot
far away from urban
gridlock, rant and rave.
Pollution is unknown.

It is unlikely, however, that Guff
will quit his rented cave.

Guff believes
a man should only go so far
in search of peace.

If he fails to find it
he must settle for
small traumas of ordinary, daily war,

which comes dropping quick
on rich and poor, young and old, well and sick.

Story

'There was a crash on the Galway road
at two this morning. Seven dead.'

'That'll make a great story,' she said.

shedding a question

Guff studies the lone seagull
in the Atlantic.
The bird is washing himself
(how does he know it's a he?)
Wings lift, fall, perform in the waves.
Neck is a white jewel in the sun.
Beak works overtime, piercing
feathers, reaching flesh.
The seagull jumps, settles, jumps,
The sun collaborates.
All great washing is a collaboration.
The Atlantic is pleased to pay attention.
It's a long time since Guff
saw one of God's creatures
enjoying himself so much.
Good Lord, mutters Guff, this is pleasure.
What have I lost?
When did I last
know pleasure like this?
Where is my beak?
Where are my wings?
Where is my private Atlantic?
When did this seagull know stress?
When was it bullied by time?
Why am I so unaware,
so impotently disconnected
from what I might learn
from my body?

Why am I thinking like this?
Why can't I mind my mind?
        The seagull
flashes its white jewel in the sun,
folds, unfolds its wings,
enjoys the Atlantic,
does a job on itself,

is clean

and then

rises
into a sky that is pleased
to accommodate its flight,
shedding a question to Guff:
Watchful old boy,
What are you up to, tonight?

Knowledge

When his heart, like the world is
            witchtit dry
Guff knows not to look the sun
            in the eye.

When water drips in his mind like
            Chinese torture
he has five Bewley's buns with
            marmalade and butter.

When he knows he's standing on
            shifting sand
he listens to the storyteller from
            Hawk Island.

When the Hawk Island storyteller loses his memory
Guff plants in his mind a new story.

When the story flies in a thousand directions
Guff knows the power of vital concoctions.

Sun, water, sand and story
know Guff is waiting, willing and ready.

The extent

The extent of his not knowing
hammers Guff now and then,
causing him to look with wonder
at those creatures he calls other men

until his mind and flesh
combine to creep

like banished snakes through countries
Guff can't begin to know

and he asks himself

How deep is the Shannon near Limerick?
Why does the average jeep remind him
of the hunchback of Notre Dame?
What is it like to die in your sleep?
How did I forget the name
of the man who said life is a dream?

The extent of his not knowing
says 'Don't worry how deep the Shannon is.
It's flowing.'

the colours of heaven

I will never come to you, Guff me lad,
unless you're willing to go dripping mad.

Guff says nothing. The voice knows well
Guff will scratch the skin of the possible

and if it bleeds, well, look and see
what it means to the voice, to you, to me.

Guff and the voice sometimes go to war,
accounts of which are brief and rare

written in the dark where the voice and Guff
agree that neither should be too stiff

to go dripping mad on a summer's night
when the colours of heaven banish dark and light.

a vibrant time

in the island of corners
peace
is a moment of rest
between murders

Guff loves such moments
prays
they may yet fill his nights
and days

stands on a clifftop
looks at the sea
if waves were peace peace peace
let them break over me

let me drown there a while
rise to the light
at last know the difference
between love and hate

in a vibrant time
relax be aware
who I may choose to be
all I may dare

Guff at coffee

What do you wish to do?
I'd like to grow.

Why do you talk?
Words help me to know
a little.

Did you ever kiss your father?
No.

What have words given you?
A view from below.

What do you see from there?
Some peace. Much war.

Who will win?
No one.

bullets

Words are bullets. Guff is a target.
Sometimes, Guff shoots to kill.

Words hide behind windows, wait
for Guff riding past on his bicycle,

Dallas his skull
with bland assassin skill.

Guff gets up, recovers, sinks
into coffee or Jameson, and thinks.

Opportunity comes like Christmas.
No love, though. Guff gives a blast

of his shotgun, dagger verb at work
on the brain of some insulting jerk

who picks himself up, goes his way,
to live and fight another day.

Guff reads a poem. Yes, words at work
in another country. How come

the same words can rise and fly
like starlings in a September sky

bringing magic to a muddy road.
Words are strange, like the ways of God.

Guff returns to guffing
viewing all from below,
stumbling now between real joy
and real trouble.

He keeps an eye out. You never know
if you're out or in,
                victim or assassin.

Little bullets lie in wait,
tickets to the Golden Gate.

Little bullets cough and spit
neat as proverbs when they hit.

And little bullets take their time
to polish a curse or kill a poem,
despatch you to Hell or open the Kingdom.

the grey old badger's head

Guff breathes on the radio
heavily, speedily, guffing about
the soul.

Lettie Pryce said later
'Guff, you talk shit.'

'Should I use my shit
to feed pigs in France?' asked Guff.

'Do what you like with it,' she said
'but leave the soul alone.'

'Why do you talk to me?' asked Guff.

'How can a human being
use so many words
and say so little?'

Guff scratched the head, the grey old badger's head.
'Upon my soul, I cannot say,' he said.

'And if I could say, would I tell
the truth to you, dear Lettie?
Or would I spin those lively lies
that bring the sparkle to your eyes?'

puzzled as ever

Guff walks through the graveyard
where words are buried.

He reads the headstones.
Words about words.

Starlings fly overhead.
How many words are dead?
Do their skeletons survive?

A rat scurries over graves.
hea hea hea   he says.

(That's what Guff hears anyway).

Guff says a prayer for the dead words,
for every buried story,
for thine is the kingdom the power and the glory.

Thine.
Beautiful: when where how far from here?
Water into wine.

Words, countless millions deep in the earth.
Three starlings in the sky.
Guff, puzzled as ever.
Why?

Beyond the graveyard wall,
a lazy river flowing

like the day he faced the farmers and their wives
and said the long poem
about St Patrick and Oisin.

Christian. Pagan.
Oisin: Strength in our hands.
        Truth in our hearts.
        Deeds expressing words.

And Saint Patrick giving out
to the great pagan.

Guff hears the words across the years,
across languages, across the sight
of starlings enjoying the sky

as if their flying silence will never die.

Flash

Darkness gathers itself like an untold story.
Guff pulls the blanket over his head.
His mind is tired.
His tongue, too.
Although prone and still, he's moving
into a new country
where the lost are at home.
Sleep is another place
where he's happy to go astray.

What's that sudden flash in his closed eyes?
How many words did he speak today?
Where are they gone?

A flash of light won't trouble a sleeping man.

The path of totality

She tosses her hair for fun.
Guff forgets his lifelong interest
in the total eclipse of the sun.

At this moment

'Irony is a kind of cowardice,' she said
'the kind of thing that has no place
in heaven or in bed.'

Is Guff an ironist, she'd like to know.
Well, at this moment,
No.

walls of silence

Guff stands at the door of a house of silence.
It must be forty years since a word
was spoken there. Two swallows
flash in and out of where was once
a window. Their wings are small thunder.
The house preserves its silence like a treasure.

Guff puts his right hand on the brown door.
His fingers run along the cold wood.
Fifty years ago a dark-faced woman
gave the lie to those who said that she
was vain, frivolous, and lacked stamina in bed.

Her words are engraved on the walls of silence.
So are the words she spoke of Kitchener, Stinkinner,
'stench of the devil, better far,' she told
her children, 'to be a patient rebel, get
all your songs in order for those not born yet:
A patient self knows rebellion is never too late.'
Guff lets the silence penetrate his fingers,
enter his blood and bones. This is a cold place.

She said that silence, if allowed to live,
would wake the soul in many a withered face.
Guff hears the silence in the dwindling light,
marvels at the part it plays in swallows' flight.

flesh

Tigers live on flesh
(Guff listens, hears a voracious roar)
and the Celtic Tiger lives
on the flesh of the poor.

The Celtic Tigress, too
is a ravenous bitch.
Guff wonders about the day
she'll chew the flesh of the rich.

Here skip the starving Tiger Cubs
scrunching munching this and that
and her and him and it and them,
Chloe, Jack, Diana, Pat.

God bless the Tiger family
who know that greed is good,
that human flesh is everywhere
like human blood.

Tiger Tigress Tiger Cubs
are a happy family,
role models for all boys and girls
who must climb the tree.

From the top of the tree, tired eyes look down
at Guff, who is not a climbing man
but who loves to consider the playful sky
which, like himself, may laugh or cry
or, failing that, ponderwonder why.

pet

Evening, late evening, hummed Guff in her ear,
cold evening threatening mad weather.
If we're going to stop at all
we'd better stop now
        as the pet said
                to his mother.

At some point

Amanda Barry introduced
the short back and sides
into the British Army,
Amanda was a man,
well, dressed as a man
'cos no woman was allowed
near the British Army
at the time.
With the short back and sides
Amanda got rid of British Army lice
and had a baby
by Lord Somerset.
That's how Amanda was found out.
Needless to say, says Guff,
she was a Cork woman.
She had a heart and a half
and she defeated
an ignorant world, the kind
of world that dominates, prospers and thrives
in various guises.
Sometimes, says Guff, I think it might be a good idea
if we all had a change of sex
at some point in our lives.

Imagine a day in Tigertown
when all wives are husbands,   husbands, wives.
Fuggy's Dinner Party made £400,000
IRA Ceasefire Is Selective
Top Model Milovic raped as she slept
Soldiers kill their Comrades
Are you a Saver or a Squanderer
Outcry as no place found for potential rapist
Black Market Offers Rich Returns to Gangs
The Real Crocodile Dundee Goes Gaga
Four Teenagers killed in Donegal
Billionaires are a girl's best friend.
Sex for sale... read the small print
Just one more cross to bear
Bid to increase TDs' salaries has little popular support
Woman attacked by hitchhiker
By-pass to proceed at snail's pace
Bookies deem tax-cut a good bet
Squeeze Tourists till the pips squeak
Animals can teach us a trick or two
Two Corkmen are better than three
American Teenagers opt for Chastity

Nothing says

If they should assault you, dear,
Know that you are welcome here
in Guff's deep unprogressive cave
where shadows gather, rape and rave
in every corner of Guff's head
packed with the living and the dead.
But if, my dear, you suffer wrong
from bad old men or thoughtless young,
come and talk to scratchy Guff

until you know you've had enough
of talking to his patient face
not without its trace of grace
so that your hurt is not as deep
as when it stabbed you in your sleep
and followed you no matter where
you picked your way in the open air.
Hurt like yours goes everywhere
and deepens with each passing year.
Guff knows that; and that is why
he listens, looks you in the eye
and takes, or seems to take a part
of your deep hurt into his heart,
lightens your load, increases his own
and still remains content to listen,
saying little, or nothing at all
whiles shadows darken every wall
of where he is content to live
and nothing says Forgive! Forgive!

conviction

I greatly fear, Guff said to the trapped
butterfly that yet could not accept
the freedom he offered it,

there's no other option now
but to offer you the new moon,
the dark, the midnight cold

and the conviction hoisted on me
that no matter how I try to tell your story
it will, like mine, never be told.

a certain yearning

Guff listens to her.
He's learning.
She knows everything that can be known
about modern art,
post-modern poetry,
feminism, futurism,
post-humanism, post-apocalyptic mesmerism.
She's generous, she gives
all her knowledge away
for free, the gift
of infallible authority.
She's twenty-three.
Guff looks, listens, recognises
a certain yearning
that from an early age
he associates with learning.
Quickly, he scratches his head
and hangs on every word
intensely, sweetly.
Pierpoint never hanged a man
more neatly.

Sauntering

Guff went sauntering all day among
the sick and sad and other
human ingredients of song
circussing in his head.
The cave ceiling was a blue sky.
'I don't see much point in dying,' he said.

Guff hopes

The word is the world
without the L
without the hell

Guff hopes
with the help of the dove and the eagle
and every forgotten soul
to harvest it well,

to comfort the afflicted
feed the hungry
touch the lonely

give a song
to Christy Thorne
in his latest cell.

He loves them both

Guff has a fountain pen
and a black biro.

He loves them both.
They let him flow
at a time when spiritual
constipation is all the go.

A fountain
pen
lets flow the names of stars
and distant cousins
on the blank page of his mind.

A black
biro
tells why a daring madness
rather than a tedious security
suggests a hero.

Not that Guff uses his black biro
and his fountain pen
all that often
but when he does
he has the hope of being
a starry earthy spermy rivery man
a flowing animal creature beast

the last of the fabulous Foxrock brothel keepers
making nineteen and a half million pounds per year
out of the cunts and pricks
of Tigertown.

Guff asked himself

Guff heard the disciple and the disc jockey
discussing the telling of secrets
playing of prerecorded music
effects of changing to a different colour
sourceless agitation of mind
special lighting effects
how to receive instructions from another
the most suitable place for untrammelled dancing
and how to learn from misfortune and suffering.

Afterwards, Guff asked himself
which of the two he might choose to be
(if he had to).

He couldn't honestly say.
The nature of the choice puzzled him at the time
and does, increasingly, to this day.

now and then

There's an innocence of heart and mind
that Guff has lost
though now and then, when he's unaware,
it steals back into his spirit
and lights a happy fire.

green graffiti

Once again, it is the strangest thing:
the word is hovering beyond his mind,
beyond his fingers.
Stranger than the strangest thing, then,
to come upon a child
(is he ten?)
scrawling on a wall –
      Ginnie Burns
      sucked in Fitzer Glynn
      and blew him out
      in bubbles. Is that a sin?

Bubbles. That was it. Fitzer Glynn.
Ginnie Burns blew him out in bubbles.
Is that a sin? Venial? Mortal?
Grievous matter, perfect knowledge, full consent.
Is that what the man in black meant?
Bubbles?

      The long straight street stretches away.
Refugees loiter here and there.
An old man talks to a bottle.
The Turk is looking for a fiver.
The child (is he ten?) stands back,
      admires his green graffiti.

Guff follows a path
      beyond his mind
            beyond his fingers
                  sees things change.
The evening light is drunk,
it totters on the edge
of dark crack-up.
Guff keeps going.
What else is there to do?
Why will he never achieve

the freedom of green graffiti?
Why will he never stand back from a wall,
hands on hips, and admire
his own scandalous mythology?
Why is growing up
a growing down?
But he keeps going, grumpy Guff
    sniffing the flying words
        of Tigertown.

Gazebo

Out of the darkened lane
close to where
the Gazebo Cinema
flashed magic
to young and old

small whispered words of love

reach Guff, he can
hardly believe them,
stands still a moment,
eats and drinks
the words,
then, strangely satisfied
yet emptier than ever,

moves slowly through the rain
saluting Marilyn, Audrey,
Groucho, Hopalong
and gruff John Wayne
roughing his drizzly head

where whispered words
climb, stumble, fall,
regroup, totter, stand,
cascade,

whispered words, piercing,
most piercing words of all.

What did she say? She didn't say.
She whispered
He heard
every little word
in the fabulous dark
where the sun is happy to set,

tiny whispered words in the dark
Guff will never forget.

Calm

Very calmly, she tells Guff
the pain is terrible, it hit her
at work and won't go away,
a coward beast here to stay
struck without warning.

Calmly, too, she tells Guff
that when the drugs work
she lies in bed, wide-eyed in the dark,
goes to Mass with Mozart
at four in the morning.

For the moment

Guff lets himself walk with himself
talk with himself
about sore toes and sudden
pains in his back and teeth.
He enjoys these conversations with himself
and when an argument begins
he's happy to win and lose.
When victory and defeat are inseparable
he drinks vodka with success and failure
and will not choose.
How can you choose between one and the same? he asks himself.
Himself replies, what is your name?
Guff, says he. What's yours?
Guff.
Where were you baptised?
In a chapel among trees.
Where were you confirmed?
Same place.
What was the point of the exercise?
State of grace.
Do you live in that state?
I was sinned into exile.
Is that where you are now?
Yes.
Who's with you?
You.

What shall we do today?
Walk, talk, share coffee and brown bread.

　　　　Guff walks with himself.
They're silent now. For the moment, enough said.
The moment is happy despite either side.

shadow kingdom

The killer threatens the boy, tells him
to go to England or be shot.
Guff walks in the shadow of Mountjoy.
The shadow says, 'Thou shalt. Thou shall not.'
The boy has twelve hours to leave his home.
He leaves. Mountjoy. London. Liverpool. Paris. Rome.
Guff talks to himself in his shadow kingdom.
Isn't that, he asks himself, what most folk do?
'That's true,' himself replies. 'That's true.
What will you do, Guff, if the killer talks to you?'

The Belfast Train

When London Bridge was falling falling down
                falling down
Guff met Mother Goose
                on the train from Belfast,
charming lady full of bells
                with a taste
for prawns pasta Virgin olive oil.
                She gobbled them fast,
so fast that Guff had never seen food
                so quickly lost.
The train flashed through winter fields
                white with frost
and London Bridge was falling down falling down
                falling down so fast
Guff had a closer look at Mother Goose,
                her eyes surpassed
all his dreams visions expectations,
                they expressed

centuries of torture, screams, mockeries,
        they laid waste
the hopes of children, mums, dads,
        Guff reeled from the blast
of evil emanating from the lady
        with a past.

That's when Jack Frost came in the window
        of the Belfast train
and said that for the children's sake
        joy would oust pain
though London Bridge was falling down falling down falling down
        and the wolf still killed the lamb
Jack Frost gave new words into the hands
        of Mother Goose,
she held them high, examined them, and sang
        the new words gaily,
Yes, London Bridge is falling down falling down falling down
        my fair lady
but we'll go for a stroll through London Town
        be it dry or rainy
and we'll cross the Bridge as the sun goes down
        on Tom Dick and Harry.
If Mother Goose takes a shine to Jack Frost
        the merry pair may marry
and so be rid of the longing pain.
Guff takes a shine to the Belfast train.
some journeys must be made again.

Corncrake

Once, in the heyday of his youth,
    Guff reviewed a book.
Now, in the heynight of his age,
    he cherishes the mistake.
The dusty tome is laughing at Guff,
    scratchy rheumatic corncrake.
Crake! Crake! Crake! A cry
    where no one bothers to look
though now and then, it must be said,
a passing listener cocks his head
and hears, or looks as if he heard
an unpolluted, solitary word
    through green fields shining,
such a word as may have been
    in the beginning.

Such a creature

The massive black cat stretches across the sky
from Foxrock to Scartaglin.
Guff gapes, wonders
how such a creature
darkens so much of the world without,
claws the world within.

Youth itself

Guff halts, looks at the roses,
the red roses.
They are youth itself,
the earth loves them
as Guff does.
The notion of picking one
makes him feel like a killer
turning people to skeletons.
His eyes pay homage a while,
then he walks
across gravel and stones,
roses sweetening his mind,
youth laughing in his bones.

black eyes black

The way that bastard beats his wife, she said,
I see her with two black eyes black
down the two sides of her face.
      I will pray for a malediction
            on his head.
      I will ask heaven to make him
            know pain till he's dead
and after he's dead, if possible.
      I hope his arse shuts
like a trap-door and the shit breaks out
            through his eyes and mouth.
      I want him to know in himself
            the pain he's inflicted
              on her.

But would she want the same thing?
      That's what amazes me.
She'd probably make an excuse for him.
      She's the kind of woman
who'd forgive the worst cruelty
      of the crassest bastard imaginable,
            I try to understand her
but I can't, for the life o' me.
      The more savage he is
the more excuses she makes for him.
It really drives me mad, trying to understand.

I can't. I can't. Can you?

Guff said no.

clown

So when Paddy from Clare swore
he'd never see the Banner County again
but would spend the rest of his days
walking up and down Mrs Hennessy's lane

listening to the old woman's black stories
of drownings accidental and planned,
of judges being bribed over rights of way
and murder over card-games and strips of land,

Guff knew the value of exile
from others, from himself, from now,
now above all. He might grow
out of this, even begin to develop a style

walking with the stranger full of rage
and gentleness, bullying himself along
the potholed road while Wards and McDonaghs
who'd once revelled nights of drink and song

tooled up with chains hatchets hammers
axes knives bats stones on the edge of a town
where only one would die, hundreds laugh,
and Guff walk the tightrope of the exiled clown.

the trick

Guff comes near to choking at times
     not just with fishbones and chickenbones
        certain words do the trick

words in prose words in funny rhymes
     words that look quiet but know how to scream
words that thump the gut and make him sick

You should see Guff trying to steer clear of these
     he's like a deer being watched by a tiger
with a view to demolition and sustenance

he's like a ten-year-old at the back of the class
     waiting to be set upon by a serious teacher
because he hasn't a clue about linguistic resonance

''Twould be better for all of us if you
quit school today, you're not fit to sweep
the streets, like your father before you.'

When Guff starts choking he opens his gob and screams
Screams are as healthy as a seaweed bath.
Certain words, for the moment, leave his dreams

alone.

A fly

Guff goes to Mass,
Kneels, prays.
When the moment comes to say
'Peace be with you'
to his neighbour
he offers his right hand
to the person nearest him
who says
'Piss off! I don't shake hands with strangers.
For all I know, you might have been
pickin' snot from your nose with those fingers
or up to how-do-you do in the loo
without washin' afterwards.
No, sir, your paw is not for me.'
Guff shrivels into himself,
becomes a fly banging wings and head
against a shut window
in a garden shed
attached to a Convent of Mercy.
The fly bangs its head and cries
Mercy mercy mercy mercy
until it can cry no more
and drops exhausted
on the tolerant floor.

maybe, maybe

When Guff feels stupid
he sits and broods on his mistakes
his gross inabilities
his laughable lack of talent
his alienation from techniques
his estrangement from the crudest concept of style
his ludicrous attempts at communication
his sad non-relationship with grammar
his old dog-like smelly slavish
disconnection from words
his five gammy senses
non existent sixth
his eyes puffed bloodshot things

but fit for brooding on

which he does he does
until, perhaps around four in the morning,
the silence is broken by a drunken refrain
in English or Irish or Italian
a woman emits a perfect scream
of post-pub ecstasy
a lover responds with a Temple Bar call

Guff pours himself a glass of legal poteen

not bad

maybe, maybe

not irredeemably stupid after all.

A crucial part

A crucial part of Guff's stupidity (he believes)
                is how quickly he forgets
                        whatever is important
                                or significant.

He longs for somebody to tell him why
        any person place or thing
                is important
                        or significant.

He waits. Nobody comes. If someone comes
        and tells Guff why,

        he'll be forever in their debt.

                Till then,
a crucial part of Guff's stupidity
        is his compulsion to forget.

He knew

He heard a sonnet once. Got up. Went walking.
Heaven has the oddest ways of talking,

not to mention singing. If you do
you'll sonnetsing till you are black and blue

like Guff slouching down the Limbo Road,
his rhythm breaking, as he knew it would.
So many broken rhythms sing in his blood
like the daft, dying leaves of Autumn God.

The killing silence

Certain birds, like certain words, are dying out.
Soon they will be heard no more.
Guff will test the killing silence
in meadow, laneway, cliffwalk, hill and slope
Resonant places once. Now, nothing there.

rough draft

All day in the echoing cave
the bee circles Guff's head
like a lecture on metaphor
like a story he doesn't want to know
like retelling a bad dream
like a murderous review
like a China Wall phone call
like a series of inexplicable giggles
like unconfirmed rumours
or nuggets of scandal over coffee

or like that interminable wait at the yellow door
despite the fact that Isobel swore

she'd be down in a jiffy.

Guff offers this jiffy to the bee.
The bee continues to buzz in robust scorn
as if the buzzing were his way of saying
                    that Guff
is bluffing the world of men and women
with his pretended existence,

a semi-articulate shadow,
    Guff the rough draft

    not fully born.

  Away from the bee
    away from all eyes
      slyly he dreams
        what it means

   to be here
   or there

walking a beach, tide going,
sand darkened, shell-evidence everywhere,
and Guff exploring the world in a chair,

    a rough draft of a man
waiting to be re-written
with skill and love and care.

A conference of birds

Guff went to Trabranafairrge for a week
lived on periwinkles and brown bread
but more than that he wanted to find out
how long he'd be able to live in his head.
He shut up, looked at shells and seaweed,
pondered a dolphin having fun,
said never a word, not even when his toes bled
on rocks or his ceiling admitted rain.

Then, 'Is this a joke?' a seagull asked him
flying perilously near his silent breast.
'Piss off,' roared Guff, the bird of heaven
wheeled and sought the refuge of its nest

high on the cliff where a conference of birds
discussed ways of robbing food for their young.
Silence is golden, periwinkles are OK
but Guff broke out in a word-besotted song.

Guff the collector

The silence of the infinite spaces
is a cosmic black plastic bag
waiting for words to be dumped in it.

Nothing terrifying about that
if word is a bomb
blowing silence to pieces.

You can pick up the pieces anywhere.
Guff collects them
like brown or white pebbles on a shore,

like stamps quickly out of date,
like verses of old songs everyone seems to have forgotten
apart from a few burning lines of love or hate

that spring to life when Guff sings them aloud
slouching the Limbo Road through the goingplaces crowd
gaping at the first man that cool evening
when he went for a walk with God.

the mere mention

Guff met Jamie the day of his Confirmation.
Jamie had decided to take Marmaduke
as his Confirmation name
now that he was a soldier of Christ
                although
          not many years later he told Guff
the mere mention of love
was enough to make him puke.
Nevertheless, he still signed himself
          Jamie Xavier Marmaduke.

Meals

Black coffee and stories of corruption
are Guff's breakfast.

For lunch, a sandwich and scandal.

For dinner, a slice of the salmon of ignorance
and a resinous meditation on the day's evil.

For a midnight snack, a cherry muffin
and a glass of sympathy with midnight
for turning black.

Guff stumped forever

Guff sat in the dark and tried
to remember her voice. He tried.
He couldn't summon it.

If he heard it, he'd recognise it.
Between the remembering and the summoning
stretched one more desert of longing.

If he heard the voice say one word
he'd feel the years were justified
but the desert laughed at his efforts.

A laughing desert is a merciless thing.
It defines what may and may not be done.
It sneers at the sun.

It stretches away into itself
like a joke that will never end.
It turns the sky into mockery of sand.

Maybe her voice is buried there.
Guff sits in the darkness of his cave,
eyes closed. Darknesses touch each other

like lovers who know the meaning of one
and recognise the moment
when the union will come undone.

But will they say it?
Will it take years to break?
And her voice to be a revealing shock?

And Guff to forget not just every word
but the voice that uttered them?
The scale of what is forgotten

is no easier to measure than grains
of sand often compared to stars
blinking and winking like randy youngsters

sizing each other up in city pubs
or summer beaches or raving places
where one voice becomes countless voices.

Thank heaven for forgetfulness,
Thank heaven for mocking oblivion,
for darkness copulating with darkness,
for Guff stumped forever by a lost voice.

All he will say

Guff suffered a heart attack.
It wasn't frightening at all.
He saw a beautiful gentle lady in black
who said, 'Come on, dear Guff,
let's get on the pig's back.'

The pig's back was smooth and even
like the sand around the Virgin Rock
like the skin on Vanessa Cole's shoulder and neck
like a quiet sideroad in heaven.

How long did Guff stay on the pig's back
with the gentle beautiful lady?
He will never know the answer to that
because he threw time over a hedge.
All he'll say is that a blasted heart
may be the source of shocking privilege.

Again, true

She couldn't bring herself to say the word
though it was eating her.
Instead, she talked of apples and hurling,
attempts to play the guitar,
exploits of a wild young brother.

Guff listened to her. He knew
that he too was beaten. He said
true. Again, true. What other word
may be said when a woman
is being eaten?

Wet

Guff knows Shakespeare said that mercy
droppeth like the gentle rain from heaven
but where's the comfort in that beauty
on a merciless pissing day in Dublin

when every body and soul in the place is wet?

Questions

Possession is the grave of love, she said,
Every true lover is a loner.

Guff scratched his questions:
Was I ever an owner?

If possession is the grave of love
is dispossession the womb of hate?

Is every true hater never alone
but scaffolded by strong women and men?

And is that strength pathetic,
deluded and sick?

Put your questions back in their cage, she said,
and stretch in the freedom of bed.

And she laughed

When she stuck her tongue in Guff's mouth
he seemed to choke into eloquence
beyond the world of sense.

He tasted the sea.
He tasted the eagle's beak.
He tasted the meaning of free.

And she laughed as she passed
out through the morning light
dressed in liquid black and white

laughing like a gift that doesn't care
who nurtures or abuses it in the end.
Rarer than rare she is, thought Guff. Rarer than rare.

Once, there was a photograph

Someone kicked the shit out of The Rapist last night.
His face is black, blue, bloody, green
Like the flag of an unknown country.
People glance at him like he's a disease.
He can scarcely walk.
They call him The Rapist and they don't know why.
He's a target for moralists
out for a feelgood kill.
He hasn't tuppence to his name.
Black, blue, bloody, green.
A woman crosses herself as she passes him.
Guff gives him the price of a meal.
He walks or half-staggers down the street,
a hungry, spent, spat-on Tigertown leper.
Once, there was a photograph of him in a paper.
How much tiredness can plague a man's eyes
before the city dies?
Where will it be buried?
What will a predator bother to save?
Will The Rapist kneel and pray at the grave?

The way

The way the man said 'money'
and again 'money'
Guff knew the meaning of money:
      Cinderella's Ball
             Caesar's secret itch
                    stupefied youth
                            vain age
      and the oldest religion of all
with ardent converts at its beck and call.

Paradise

Lettie Pryce stands back and looks at Guff
noting the scratched nut, the practiced scowl.
She says, 'After fifty years of breathing in this world
why wouldn't your breath be foul?
To be fair, however, I must admit I've met
a few good men with evil breath.'

'Have you now?' says Guff. 'Well, then, may God
protect you from evil bastards whose breath is good.
And furthermore, dear Lettie, may you perfect the art
of enjoying the Evesmell
of your own most reluctant fart.'

'Thank you,' says Lettie. 'Still one thing we both know is true:
Adam had a sweeter smell than you.'

'How do we know that?' asks Guff.

'A man's bad smell' says Lettie 'is enough
to make any woman opt for hell.
Some women do.

How long, I ask myself, would I
stay in even a perfect garden with you?

'That's for you to decide' says Guff.
'I'm not into gardens.
And I know nothing of perfection.'
'You're at the point of no return' says Lettie,
giving him the mocker's eye.
'Anyway, enough o' smells,' she says.
'How would you like some ice-cream
and a slice of apple-pie?'

'You take my breath away' says Guff.
He sighs, 'Apple pie and ice cream?
Paradise.'

Affection spars with mockery in Lettie's eyes.
Guff will never know
the source of the sudden, perfect
knockout blow.

Final page

Be on the side of the forgotten
Lettie says to Guff.
Find a word for those who've no word to say.
You're that last page in a book
it took a lifetime to write.

> Any last page
> deserves a finer word
> than Guff can manage tonight.
> Money is holy.
> Money is shite.
> Money is Ireland now.

Something about money wants to murder men and women
as Guff hears them among the forgotten.
Words perish on painted lips,
come to life in the raw spittle
of love or curse.

Guff tries to remember those to whom he never gave
A second thought. His cave is free
of such ghosts. No second thought. No word.
Nothing between the first and final page.
Somewhere, he knows, there's a word that matters,
echoing through forgotten hearts.
He will scour himself for it
and never find it.

He will know
hate and frustration, fear and rage.
He will hear laughter too
cutting through black bars, tall trees,
walls, clocks, timber, books, windows,
the final page,
to reach the forgotten.
He will sit there like a prodigal son
silent, humpy, free,
as close to home as he is ever
likely to be.

Sorry

Guff, brief visitor, stands at the door,
says to his friend 'I'm sorry,
I can't stay any longer,
please excuse me, I must leave now, I had
a few great lies to tell you.'

Guff to the women

Go out, good women, stroll the streets
      Then come back home and wash.
All your clothes have been stolen
      And the Corkman has the cash.

It's time to dance, it's time to prance,
      What else may a woman do
When her knickers and bra are in Ballina
      and her skirt is in Katmandu?

Stories

A treatise written by the hangman Pierrepoint
shows law-abiding man
how to train birds of prey
and catch falling stars
without burning their feathers
in the elemental fire.

Also, the hangman presents
an emetic made
      from the essence of hemp
to make the Ants of Peru
      vomit up the gold
they have swallowed lump
      by shining lump.

Guff knows these stories are old
treats them with respect
      passes them on
          to men,
fleas, cats, ferrets, lice, spiders, dogs, ducks and crows
      and a million Americans
enjoying St Patrick's Day in Dublin.

Rescue

In the beginning was the word.
We learned to use it, abuse it
till it cried for mercy.
When we had no mercy
the word recovered all on its own
and had mercy on us
      who went on using
         abusing
till we lost sight
of the small bird and the white paper,
the thin dark lines that rescued us
from frightening talk of art
     and thick, vindictive ice
        blocking the heart.
The word broke the ice, the icy bits
became water we drank
and washed our bodies in
from beginning to end.
Somewhere, under threatening clouds,
we had to admit
the word was our friend.
      Even then
we used abused and had no mercy.
There was no end to the word's mercy,
no end that we could see.
Will it be like this forever?

Or will there come a moment
when the word will abandon us,
cease to be
and we
won't ever know how to say
the word has fled
because our tongues are the tongues
of the wordless dead.

Born

Guff was born without a word to his name.
He had no name
but his mum and dad rooted about
in rumours of uncles and grandfathers
and came up with Guff
Guff
who would grow up
go down, now and then,
learn to listen to sober and drunk
men with lines of work in their hands,
listen
to words of teachers and priests,
footballers, fishermen, blacksmiths
describing the hooves of horses,
listen
to stories of ghosts in the quiet byroads
where lovers strolled away from inquisitive eyes,
listen
to words that were puzzling and clear at the same time,
words
dancing like flies on the brown tide
that sometimes knew how to rough it,
words
that seemed like keys to love and a pound in your pocket,
words that violated silence late at night
then went away like emigrants
taking the bus to the boat or the plane,
words
that played strange games
with his laughter and loneliness,
took him by the hand in the midst of nightmare
gave him peace for a while
before war was declared
and he heard the suffering cries
for which there were no words
as he lay in the dark

and listened, listened, waited
for gifts the darkness might bring,
words
that crawled crept climbed
fell, rose up,
and began, like small birds
greeting the morning, to sing
for a brief deep heavenly while.
Silence, then. Silence and gratitude.
And what was the word
for the gift of darkness,
the unspoiled, primal style,
the innocent, open, vital style
born of nothing, capable
of telling all?

Let Guff come coughing

How's she cuttin'? High and low
The North wind lacerates Pimlico.
The times are greedy. Give us time
And we'll dream up a novel crime
that criminals never even dream
though their sentences rip and scream.
Good editors will buy and sell
two cups of gold, fresh out of hell
while the dope-eyed hitmen swagger
dreaming of the perfect dagger
not of our times. Agamemnon, Hector
stole the prayer-book of a Sligo Rector.
At such times, you know it's tragic
that apes turn into men through logic.

Consider, then, the power of Art
that can make a poem out of a fart,
How's she cuttin'? Guff asks again
in a tone that's sweet and nice.
Thick and hard, like a landlady's slice,
is the reply. Give the poem of Art to men,
let poets be rich, moneymen poor,
take pity on the freezing whore,
give language a rest from human gobs,
dress beggars up in Bishops' robes.

Let Guff come laughing from his cave
at the lies of life, truth of the grave.
Hairy corpses don't need to shave
but the living must be razorsharp
before they dance to an angel's harp.

to talk

When Guff began to talk, talk,
    Terror trampled peace
Mackerel in bags of ice
    Prayed heaven for release.
Old Foxtrot cocked his head to hear
    Two mermaids telling why
They'd never sleep with snoring poets.
    In fact, they'd rather die.
Mermaids, even on the rocks, don't lie.

An honest man

When the fisherman drowns the cod
And priests play football with young God;
When the farmer grows to love the fox
And Dublin's virgins fit in a box;
When the mackerel frightens the shark
And the crow outsings the lark;
When the Bishop quits his palace
To wander wonderland with Alice;
When the Moneylender aims to be fair
And the Politician feeds the Tinker ...

When Dublin and Cork fall deep in love
And honeymoon in Ballyduff;
When Hackballscross and Kinnegad
Win a prize for not going mad;
When Thomas Street and old Blackpitts
Open the prisons and free the wits;
When Dorset Street and cold Mountjoy
Compel the girl to bridle the boy;
When Killarney Street twists and grieves
For the lack of knackers, hitmen, thieves;
When one day passes without greed
Pouring from hearts – see how they bleed;
When nun and whore, scribbler and vandal
Taste a breakfast not laced with scandal;
Then, by fish, by birds, by marzipan,
Guff will be an honest man.

When strawberries in January
Flourish on the bushes
When passion flares in February
Until the snowman blushes
When crows sing sweet in every street
When rocks get up and move
When whiskey falls instead of sleet
Then Guff will fall in love.

When berries in the month of March
Are succulent as June,
When sparrows with mad seagulls perch
And rats to badgers croon,
When Hannibal gets the OBE
And a snake outflies a dove
And Mona Lisa licks a flea
Then Guff will fall in love.

A return

Guff studies the seagull.
Never did he see
such passionate attention paid
to human or inhuman body,

such vigorous commitment
to its own happy plight,
such resolution to eradicate
whatever interferes with flight.

fisheye

'The night before, she was
me mother, me wife and me whore.
Next day, in Dame Street,
she gave me the fisheye,' he said.
'I nearly dropped dead.
How do I prove I exist?
I think I'll get pissed.'

Newsflash

Someone threw the paper on the street.
Ignorance? Perception? Giving or taking a sign?
Guff stirs the paper with his left foot.
There's nothing more forgettable than a headline.

a wave

Guff looks out the cave window
sees a black cloud sheltering a snake
hears a bell falling like rain in dark lanes
sees a picture of Christ full of pain
holes, wounds, stabbings, ruts and, to hell with you,
hears talk of money, Ireland's real religion
goes to the Point where the Sabine women
strut what's left of their wares
        and he sees
a wave gathering far out in the Atlantic
gathering like the revenge of the dead
like the new might of those who
never had a voice until now
like the resurrection of buried myths,
like the disappeared the ignored the lost
the murdered the raped the shot-on in the street
like the poems of those who will never be heard

        a wave

drowning the isle, the dear little isle
that never completely lost its ancient unkillable style
so that now, even in the state of drowning,
it will not be stuck for a song a story
a memorable spatter o' music

mesmerising all
lovers of humanheavenly sound
      from Kerry to Donegal,
        all lovers who wonder
          what did they do
            for money

        before the Fall?

A respected citizen

Guff is nowhere now.
The street has a name and there are
children playing in a cul-de-sac
each child a single sparkling star

and the barbed wire protecting the church
from exploratory vandals bent on
stealing money from the holy candles
sticks out like spikes of witty poison

and a one-legged pigeon manages to make
its way to an inexplicable crust of bread
while pertinent remarks from Mr Strindberg's
capricious diaries peck at Guff's head

but Guff is nowhere now,

nowhere, a place he has long become
accustomed to, both outside and inside,
quiet and cold, not objecting, not even wishing
to hurt, merely accommodating him
for as long as he can bear
to be a respected citizen of nowhere.

Confirmation

Guff thinks he thinks:

nothing is profound
compared to the wild metaphysics of the mind
music of the rainsound

light in and out of bed with darkness,
        deep darkness only,
confirming that when he thinks he thinks, he knows
        the heart is lonely.

sandwich

The sight of the man choking on the sandwich
(ham and cheese) is hard to bear
but there are worse curses floating
        on the Tigertown air.
Guff pulls ham, cheese and brown bread
        from the tinker's gullet
then shuffles off towards his cave.
The tinker coughs and spits in redemption.
Tigertown savours a post-midnight rave.

happy enough

Guff is happy enough when
the four o'clock in the morning blackbird sings
there's no talk of money
all God's chillun got wings

or at least are sound asleep
while darkness prepares to go
on a long journey like blind Raftery
tapping his way through the County Mayo

until he comes to that one place
where he grows young again
and never feels the need to say
why or how or when

the world craves the vision of blind men.

Don't argue

Guff loves setting out on a journey,
thrives on travelling

but not too fond of arriving.
Ask him why,

he'll mutter something
about strange faces, pigeons' wings,

phrases dropping out of the air
about third world countries,

the art of ploughing, prophecy, muck,
the old church built on a rock,

workings of the Tax Reform Code
and minor changes in the ways of God.

Don't argue. He's talking. He's alive.
Prepare. Set out. Travel. See. Hear. Arrive

but not too soon, dear hearts, no, not too soon.
Stare at that huge, original, Armstrong moon.

The snakesentence

The first time Guff saw the snake
it was a sentence wriggling across a page
so white it made snow look dark
with buried rage

Buried until now, that is. Out in the light
of yet another extraordinary day
the sentence fills all the books
in Guff's favourite library,

books of love and lust, facelift, six ways
to lose a stone in a month, London's Great Fire,
stories of the Russian Tsars, the Optimum
Nutrition Bible, Beatrix Potter and the Irish Empire.

Thousands of others, also. The snakesentence
slithers through every word of every book
behaving all the while like an apprentice
whose skills are only beginning to shape up.

That is precisely how the situation remains
and will remain for centuries to come:
it is a question of slithering through waiting brains
to bring every text into the land of dawn.

The snake never tires, the sentence never ends,
the rhythm harms itself, the meaning's never clear.
Get out of the garden, Maud, forsake your friends,
assess the poison in your chosen hemisphere.

Guff reads, re-reads, but cannot tell
how the snake became the sentence
that he can't unravel.

a clean page

Guff is the clean page of a book
made in East Timor,
bought in Dublin.
Words are written on him, in him.
He knows they're fearless,
hungry, homeless, cold.
How long will they last?
His heart is a clenched fist.
He unclenches it, fingers stretch and spread
like prayers for the dead,
sometimes flickering, rarely said.

I know

Because I walk away from love
I know that love exists.

Guff writes on East Timor:
I am a coward. Cowards persist.

I know the meaning of terror.
I know the gungho of the terrorist,
the only coward worse than me.

I'm visible, at least. Where and who is he?

The Wild Streak

May God forgive me, said Guff,
I made a killing mistake
these fifty years. I was not true
to my wild streak.

Wild streak! How do I know
I have one? Because I see, believe I see
the things I never did
yet might have done.

What is caution?
Respectability?
The coward's masks,
as far as I can see.

How far is that? If I saw
far and deep enough, would I
challenge one of the warriorforms
I notice every day in earth and sky?

Why do streets teem with reminders
of things not done?
Daring is the ultimate form of caring
for me, the man, the woman, the woman in man,

frost in sunlight, vibrations from yellow leaves,
worms half-crushed, inexplicable tears,
quick smiles, begging eyes, nightcries,
hungover faces, children and their monsters!

Opening up like a fearless flower
is the problem: when did I ever open?
Have I been shut tight as a mackerel's crack
all these years? Tell me, dear decades, what is fun?

Go for it, Guff. Go for what?
Who was that girl murdered in Cork last night?
Why did Plato hate democracy?
What does it mean to get something right?

What does it mean to let the wild streak
define and transmit its own concept of law?
Did I ever see a lawyer not wearing a suit?
Dear wild streak, what is respectability?

Why did I refuse to be educated by you,
let the dark madness sing its song,
walk the line whose nickname I forgot,
live the difference between right and wrong,

know what burning questions are
and why I must always ask them,
sitting here in the still metamorphosis
between blue and black, articulate and dumb?

This knowing is alive, it is the earth and air,
the words of that lover in nineteen-sixty-three
who cracked with me across America
and walked away laughing into her dream of Free.

It is the words I have forgotten,
the fertile country of the abundant lost,
the outrageous faces of the midnight dance,
the shocking gentleness of the kissed, unkissed,

the boy's decision to be ready to call
all shots, the girl's pursuit of music all her own,
leading her from Spain to Donegal,
making pictures of her own skeleton

exhibited under a loving oak tree,
the sharpest critic she can hope to meet.
Why, when I shuffle now, do I see
shining reminders in a long grey street?

There's the wild streak sitting on a wall,
flinging bare legs apart with laughing eyes
that will find time and space to let tears fall
and wish good luck to all lusting for paradise.

Guff has seen faces

Guff has seen faces ditched in many a street.
He has seen them in early morning light.
They hit his heart and mind in rain and sleet.

They lift to see a seagull in its flight.
They droop to watch a girl gripped by the cold
and pitiless ignorance of the night.

A world spins past on wheels of silver, gold,
so purposeful it whips Guff's breath away
as if it knew it never can grow old

but always knows the spot-on word to say
to swelling fortune kneeling at its feet.
This fortune must be grasped without delay

and gathered to the heart, sweet and complete.
Guff has seen faces ditched in many a street.

Trap

Guff knows a man who adores success, the only
wine that lifts him out of the rut.
When he can't say what others want to hear
he keeps his trap shut.

What drives a man to flatter others, to say
only words they seem to want to hear?
Seagulls fighting over bread are honest creatures,
stormy waves battering a naked shore

where a girl stood last summer before
plunging to the same sea-death as her father.
Some feelings are so true they turn love
into a decisive, calm self-killer.

This will never be a danger to the man
who knows how to flatter
and uses his whole being to that end.
God grant me, prays Guff, one friend.

Guff the reader

Famine in the culchie's gut
lives in the eyes of the Liffey rat.

Corpses strewn on Vinegar Hill
command the morningafter Pill.

Killers in the Phoenix Park
educate the morning lark.

When evening comes, the streets forget
to pay interest on the National Debt.

Guff the reader wonders who
in hell was Brian Boru

and why that Clareman took such pains
to bate the shite out of the Danes

and then make love to Ginnie Rinn
in a small bedsit in Scartaglin.

Safety

'You won more gold medals than any man in Ireland?'
'I did.'
'And where do you keep all your gold medals?'
'Under my mother's bed.'

A gossip

She gossips her way beyond the reach of friends
to achieve a reeking fame.
Using all her moist means and ends
she gives whores a bad name.

a small part

Suppose Guff knew
even a small part
of the secrets of
the eight men gathered
at the table
how would he respond
to the only man
who admits
the loneliness of night,
the emptiness
that drives him
to become
like Jimmy Spartan
in his pride
holding the whole
parish entranced
with his noble, passionate
beating
of the huge drum
the day the small bird died
and Sally Noggin ran
behind a tall wall
and cried
and cried?

She's gone

Where is Sally Noggin gone?
Is she afraid of the music she inspired?
Why are those men scouring the town for her
with such passion it seems they'll soon grow tired?

Sally's music possesses the place.
Where is her laugh? Where is her face?
Where is Sally Noggin's dark triangle?
Why has she sworn to stay forever single?

When she vanishes why does her music stay
to haunt every crevice of night and day?
All right, she's gone. She's gone.
Black midnight reels to the music of dawn.

Where?

Where would our music-lovers be,
without Bach, Beethoven, Mozart, Handel?
Where would hurling be
without Christy Ring
or football without Mick O'Connell?
And where would Dublin be
without a rich supply of scandal?

Sleeping

Guff sinks into sleep.
The Atlantic is silent.
The radio holds its tongue.
The sky is ice.
A Halloween leaf makes its way
from Pearse Street to Ringsend.
If there's a Day of Judgment
it may be like this.
Peaceful. Afterwards. Complete.
Yet anything could happen
because
it takes a few words
in an old wine cellar in Gorefield
to blow silence to pieces
and make young minds and bodies
do things
they never dreamed of doing.
Guff is sleeping.
Sleeping is a way of waiting.
Waiting marks the style of one intent on killing.
Killing happens while some are asleep
as Guff is now,
not caring when or why or how.
It happens anyway.
The happening happening happening
is a mocking proof
of the smallness of Guff's mind,
so small
the thinnest shadow
of the smallest cloud
is more than enough
to hide
behind.

Who'll ever know?

Cover the dream
       swaddled in shame.
Girl from the mountain
       what is your name?

The dream is sleeping.
       Let it lie still
Girl from the mountain
       What did you kill?

And who'll ever know
       the extent of your crime?
Girl from the mountain
       bury the dream.

almost

Guff is lost
can't say why
he almost rejoices in the logic of the bombs
that will soon obscene every sky

One November night

Guff's mind is gone up into the Dublin hills
to meet a woman who
saw a ghost stalking her one November night
and afterwards didn't quite know what to do.

Guff heard the story from a friend of hers,
a chap called Georgie Moore
who likes to make fires of piled-up yellow furze
close to his own door

because, he says, there's no excitement without a threat.
How he knows the woman Guff can't say.
If there's a way of unravelling November secrets
Georgie knows the way.

The woman

Guff's mind meets the woman in the Dublin hills,
she takes his mind in her arms
kisses it, sucks it, kisses it again
laughing at any possible threat of harm.

At this point in timelessness, it's only fair to say
that some of the woman's neighbours claim
she's the Devil's daughter and is more beautiful
than any woman you'd dare to name.

She's gifted too. After kissing Guff's mind
she takes it under a blackberry bush,
lays it in the shade of yellow sweet berries
and smiles when the mind begins to blush.

A mind blushes when it's close to heaven's door.
The Devil's daughter tells her story now
bringing the stalking ghost alive
as a leaping salmon, all tempting and raw.

The mind is eager to chew the ghost
but that phantom is a slippery lad
and fades away from woman and mind
into the waiting dark.

Who can ever know the right time to leave?
Who can say when enough is enough?
The Devil's daughter is not peevish or crass.
Guff's mind has come alive.

Is that why it slips down from the Dublin hills
back inside the scruffy old head?
Georgie Moore bids goodnight to the Devil's daughter
who smiles a smile that would resurrect the dead.

Could they but resurrect on a night like this
when small black boxes can't be found to tell
why the Boeing 727 crashed out of a cool, blue sky
and folk go on re-inventing hell.

If hell didn't exist we'd have to invent it
that the Devil in big boots and bloodred shirt
might clump the fields in pursuit of his daughter
who's trying to tell us the nature of her hurt,

the hurt embedded in her nature,
the hurt we hate to share.
Will the Devil ever retire? If he does,
let's club together to give him a rocking chair

that he may rock to and fro forever
cooing 'I don't give a damn! I don't give a damn!
Thank you all for creating and sustaining me.
I am what you are. You are what I am.'

the kind of laugh

The Devil's daughter has the greenest eyes
Guff has ever seen,
the happiest laugh
he's ever heard,
the kind of laugh
that makes him wish
he was a snake
made of ancient wiles,
milking magic
from the first word.

Only for

'My rude, gloomy, fun-hating Dad
is always stomping after me in his huge boots'
the Devil's daughter said. 'Only for my mother's love
for him, I'd swear to God he was bad.'

On the shelf

The Devil's daughter smiled and put
the Bible back on the shelf.
'You can have an evil bastard of a dad,' she said
'And be all right yourself.'

mat

The Devil's daughter on the yoga mat
stretches, bends and chants and sings
           and sings
      of virgins bleeding,
of men trying to imitate her dad,
      now and then succeeding.

She sings a song of pity for those men,
she knows her dad is sniggering,
      plain sniggering
          at men
who, if they tried, might know the joy
      of being human, now and then.

'Come sit with me,' she says to Guff
'Come stretch and bend and chat and sing
          and sing
      of bodies' wise delight.
O let the bad world go to Dad, but be
      with me all night.'

Why does the Devil's daughter bother with Guff
          when most women
      (on or off the yoga mat)
          look at him
          and laugh?

      Do they know
          what they're laughing at?

Snakes

Guff grew up with the story
that Saint Patrick had banished
all the snakes out of Ireland

so imagine his surprise when
he awoke to find a snake
wriggling through his brain

like a sprightly Dublin rumour
slithering from mouth to mouth
and a delightful sense of tumour

immortalising resonant names
the like of which you'd only find
in Dublin in the rare oul' times.

Another snake wrapped itself round
Guff's cock like a moist bandage
determined never to be unravelled

until the secret of all secrets is revealed.
On this matter, Guff's mind is calm and steady:
the secret's been revealed already.

One clever little snake with a mind
fit for the Stock Exchange
hid in Guff's armpit and found

a certain happiness there
sniffing, as only clever snakes can sniff,
for treasure in the ancient hair.

Another snake took up its abode
between the cheeks of Guff's arse,
ate his shit, drank his blood

and never once complained.
Neither did Guff complain
despite the pain.

He was all snakes now.
They wriggled inside him,
the strangest music of all,

rising and falling like dust
on Guff and his word, on all
that could be cursed or blessed

provided hell or heaven got a chance
to move closer to the snakes
writhing in their pre-Saint Patrick dance.

Guff lets them be
at peace, at war, following a process.
He lets the snakes trawl his head

until they weary and melt away
like promises of the living
or voices of the dead.

But will they ever weary?
Or will they go on thwarting the Saint
praying for a world that rarely

if ever pays him any heed
while pushy, glittering snakes
breed and prosper, prosper and breed.

Different

She looked him up and down at the Five Lamps
where cattle rabbled past in frosty steam.
Yes, she'd seen him before, closely. But where?
She eyed him. Different. Not now the man he'd been.
Were they together once? And if so, when?
She backed away. He stood, lost man among lost men.

Job

'I like my job in the Arts,' said Sara McGee
'bitchy and incestuous though it be.'

Survivors

After a grim belittling winter
        of wind and ice
                frost and rain

a tall tree stands
        near my window.
On the naked branches
        two green leaves
                remain.

Pick

All right, take your pick of languages.
The old one is magic,
a sovereign, derided icon,
the other a rough overcoat
you can wear
any icy night or biting day.
Take your pick.
You're lost, either way.
But will that stop you
saying your say?

merciless

Guff is knackered, merciless
weariness in every bone.
The word has flown.
It, too, is tired.
Even the Devil's daughter
with her divine ability
to make the most worn out
old Fortycoats of a stickin' plaster
                    dynamic and inspired

is alone.

The green moment

The green moment comes and goes
like eyes catching sight
of the nest in the tree
light on the leaf
an ambulance vanishing
a gull swerving free
a woman flinging tea out the window
two clouds becoming one
the good word from the screw
      who, on the brink of eighty,
after sixty years of prison within prison,
          discovers fun.

Bug

Guff saw the damned Millennium bug
      crawling on the floor
He whacked it with his Parnell stick
      until it crawled no more

'Welcome to the next two thousand years'
      said Guff with glinting eye
'Here's hoping they'll be better than
      the two thousand just gone by.

With wars and famines, murders, rapes
      and a billion crimes untold
is it any wonder the poor poets
      invented the Age of Gold?'

Well, bollocks to the Age of Gold,
        here's to the Age of Love instead
when old sods like me will welcome be
        into the house of God

wherever that is.' The dead bug lay
        at Guff's arthritic toes.
He stirred it with his Parnell stick
        and smelled a red, red rose

followed by a killing stink
        and then, again, that sweet rose smell
and then the oldest odour on earth:
        heaven locked in hell.

You think

You think you have it captured now
but see, it slips away
like the blackbird from the raping plough
that ruthless day.

Climbing

Half-way up Parnassus
some poets lick each other's arses.
'You include me, I'll include you.'
O immortal verses!

Higher up, you see the occasional
odd fish squatting alone
warming to the thought of flesh,
cold as a graveyard bone.

How did the poor thing end up there?
Poems floating in the air
like plastic bags in a vicious wind
once moved the heart, engaged the mind

but now they drift like battered leaves
over the every-man-for-himself land
like the lost testaments of slaves
like broken shells on Sandymount Strand

like screaming newspapers dumped in the rain
like silly talk of long ago
like dingy corners of an old brain
that no longer knows what is means to grow.

Can't stop

Guff is boring her to death
and he knows it
but he won't stop, no, can't stop.
Why does she stay in the chair
listening to this nonstop idiot?
Is she trying to guess
the original colour
of Guff's scarce hair
or is she wondering
how long she can listen
without stuffing a plastic bag
in his gob?

better get lost

Guff disappears for days on end.
All that means is that nobody bothers
to look for him. Where is he? Where
d'you think? In his cave, of course,
considering photographs of lost friends,
strangers, hungry grass, a wolf, a Chinese
girl, Brendan Behan with two black-eyes,
a horse's head by moonlight, the Pope
and several shots of the Atlantic
he sometimes goes to bed with
that he may dream of sleeping in the sea.
Don't worry. He'll be found in time,
bending down to pick smashed branches
from Bride Street after another storm
or arguing with himself about the days
when rain turns to snow,
the kind of day
when a man had better get lost
or he'll have nowhere to go.

Name

'Guff, who gave you your name?' asked the Devil's daughter.
'Moses,' Guff replied.
'Who was Moses?' she asked.
'A decent man who never lied.'

If words

If words were drops of rain
        drifting in the starry way
                turning into a downpour
                        Dublin would drown every day.

small sound

love flutters above Guff's head
like pigeons looking for bread.
If this small sound is true
love gets hungry too
shuffling from street to street
for a drop to drink, a bite to eat.

passion

She tells Guff she loves him
with a passion that brings her pain.
Guff thinks that when she speaks these words
she might as well write them on the rain.

'Just the thought of you, Guff, makes my cunt wet'
she says. 'Don't blame me for that.'
She'd be better off, Guff thinks, pouring boiling water
on a caged rat.

branches

Through Stephen's Green
on a bright frosty morning

Guff re-lives the terror
of last night's wind

seeing smithereened branches
like broken promises

scarring the ground.
He has an urge

to bend and pick them up
but he keeps on walking

because part of his mind,
remembering blood and curses,

knows that certain things are better
left behind.

Because frost is like certain forms
of politeness

Guff thinks 'hello' and
getting no reply

moves on
to say a prayer

for the poet's dead son
who, at ninety-three,

passed away in a small white room
that spoke his courtesy

unbroken by the years.
Guff signs the book

shakes the priest's hand
can't tell how many years have passed

since the old man said
'Leave a bottle of whiskey

on the mantelpiece before you go.
A man must think

at least six hours ahead
with all this threatening talk of snow.'

Papercut

Sharp paper cut Guff's finger.
He looked. Nothing. Nothing. Nothing for a while.
Then blood appeared shyly, fully
in that ceremonious bloodystyle.
Guff licked his finger clean. Clean.
There was blood again.

Blood enjoys a resurrection.
So should men,
not too frequently of course,
just now and then.

In vain

Free and lonely... Lonely and free...
If Guff ever studied philosophy
he thinks he might arrive
(after a riddled journey)
at nothing less
than the recognition
that true freedom
is the joy of loneliness.

That's what he thinks,
sitting in his chair
unable to control the capers of a single flea
Duffycircussing his hair.

In vain doth he scratch here
when the flea is there.
In vain doth he scratch there
when the agile imp is elsewhere

like the answer to some problem
mocking a philosopher.

how bad the world

The Devil's daughter knows how bad
the world can be.
That's why she sings sweet songs
of God's mercy
to Guff who's eating Bewley's bread
drinking Bewley's tea

and thinking, too, of eating
a slice of Bewley's cake
while men drop bombs on innocents

and a killer with his gun
shoots nine people praying on their knees
to the God of everyone.

a muffled room

Guff lived that winter of black ice and
children begging in the spiked streets,

a young woman gassed
in a muffled room
where walls and a picture of Harvard Yard
heard her sing
while light blighted her sight.

Who will ever separate the legend
from the real thing?

only once

So hard to find
even a hint of dooropening
in a wintry mind:
          Guff settles
for a red candle in a mug
Big Issues on the floor
a musical chirp from nowhere
a ferocious surge of gratitude
for cold, ticking solitude
          and a woman from Cork Street
          at her neighbour's door
                    screaming words
Guff only heard once before.

Zip your lip

If you've nothing to pass on
to the children,
zip your lip

like the Protestants had to do
in the twenties and thirties
of that century gone by.

Zipping the lip or making sure
you have nothing to say
has its own reward

since a zipped lip suggests
a deprived philosopher or poet.
O give him a pen or a computer

and let him have his way
with words, let him coax them
out of the dark corners

of outhouses and wet meadows,
let him rob the rats of their food,
let him learn to quote the conqueror

till he achieves the conqueror's style
of bashing a tribe into silence
till they learn how to kill

like the conqueror did
before he grew tired of conquest
and wanted a long rest

then left for home, the lyrical
village he was born in
that taught him to kick a ball,

kick it here and there on grass,
against hedge or wall, and he
sometimes shouted 'Goal! Goal!'

Who'd have thought that lad
would have taught distant souls
to zip their lips

as another style of conquest?
Guff believes we're losing touch
with the power of silence

so he pursues it in a roaring world,
nabs it now and then and sneaks it
away to his forlorn den.

What has he to say to the children,
the real judges?
The old bag's zipping his lip

and opening his ears
to the laughter of flesh and souls
in the not too dangerous streets,

opening his ears, opening his heart
to a sweet, fleeting, anarchic,
happy art,

children dancing where
there's no need for words
and words have no need for people.

Guff to his maker

Take all the lashes they give you,
the mockery they pour on your head.
The hatred they spit is proof
they're half-dead.

His maker to Guff

On, on, dear Guff, on, on, old flower,
each leg, each word
helping the other.
Let me know if you find shelter
from foul weather.

Paradise Sussed

Reading Milton, Guff hears the words of Milton's mother:
poets, like whores, only hate each other.

it was clear

Guff should never have asked directions
of the man in the pub.
Farmers don't answer strangers' questions
there. And yet he heard
John Clare was known
to be rounding the bend
when his sister heard him singing
'O Lord, won't you buy me a Mercedes Benz'

and it was clear

he'd end up in the lunatic bin
not giving a damn
for anything or anyone

except to say, all day, all night,
between gligeen bursts of laughter,
I am I am I am I am I am

chuckling

Let 'em talk, thought Guff, their envy and their hate
until they bait the badger down the side of Corrig Hill.
Lovers chuckling bedwards dark and late
keep me chuckling still.

Pretend

A sidelong glance
like a kick in the pants
can bring such pain to Guff
he raises his eyes
to the witnessing skies
and says I've had enough.
I'll pass four score
and suffer no more
from withering sidelong glances.
I'll pretend I'm a jockey
skilful and lucky
astride a mare
with the wind in her hair
conquering all the fences.

grey

What does Guff's hair say, turning grey?
The interesting thing about God?
Lets 'em all go their own way.

looking

Guff, looking out to sea and into himself,
saw a poisoned island
rising and falling
in the staggering light.

Designing Friday

At the Corner of Talkers
a man with his back to the wall
thinks he knows the story behind the hookers
this Friday. Hot secrets under her shawl

let crafty knackers think they know
of the love Batt Shanahan going blind
heaps on her and she takes with few
words. 'Batt,' she said once, 'love is a sound,
listen for it.'
Fierce common sense, her own kind
of pride, trot with her and Diarmuid
past the Corner of Talkers. She sees everything,

lets on to see nothing, scours shops, finds
what she wants, drinks two creamy pints, hears
sounds not love, shawls homewards, designing,

leaving windows and walls do the watching,
                                    listening.

Guff got it wrong

Guff got it wrong
All night he lay awake
wondering why he didn't get it right,
why in the course of an ordinary
conversation
        he could say such a thing
        to such a person
whose eyes flashed full of hurt
        and who walked

out of his life
out of his heart
forever

though of course they would meet again.

Why   why   why
rings like a harsh bell through the hours
when he should be sleeping
and in the first pitiless light
of a morning dawn

he knows he will never know
why he said those words though now
he could give himself a hundred reasons

but none would satisfy
or say
why.

The handle of the bedroom door
is the shape of the hurt
Guff will bear
from now on,

old Guff
who doesn't know,
never knew
when to keep his mouth shut
make his teeth a barrier against himself
his lips the sharpest clamper in town
his tongue a dark fish behind a rock.

There's learning to be done, he thinks, learning to be done.
Show me a man
who can say his heart without killing something
and I will be his disciple.
I'll follow him until I learn
how not to hurt.

awake

Three in the morning,
        Guff lies awake,
brooding between floor and ceiling,
        on another blustering
            out-with-it
how did-I-think-of-it – why-did-I-say-it
            mistake.

Annunciation

The words grabbed him,
announced their intentions.
He finished his travels
and buried his cat in Fatima Mansions.

A summoning music

In the middle of Mass the mobile
went off in the priest's pocket.
A summoning music commanded his head.
He grabbed the mobile.
'Call me back later,
I'm offering sacrifice,' he said.

A Battle of Poets

(FROM *The Frogs*)

The bellowing man, enraged, devours
    his rival's stylish lies.
He commissions his own terrible frenzy
    and rolls his eyes.

There follows a flashing struggle of words
    horsehair-crested, linchpins in splinters,
words chopped, clipped, man testing man,
    words charging tax-evading tinkers.

This one shakes the mane of hair on his neck,
    arranges his brows in a stormy frown,
roars, hurls words, riveted like planks,
    threatens the safety of our town.

Afterwards, seated, the pure tongue, mouth-worker,
    word-tester, lets envy flow,
feasting on the birth, life, death of words.
    It's all his lungs will ever know.

People before poetry

O balaclava in the sky
I put people before poetry.
    I always did.
If they hunger
    give them bread
and when they are no longer hungry,
    poetry.

147

No cheap houses

We have strong inward migration.
Good fortunes thrive between ceiling and floor.
My job is to say 'Watchout! Watchout!
There are no cheap houses in Ireland anymore.'

Guff tries to see precisely what changes
a lively young man into an old bore.

All the action

The note of a trumpet is eating
the heart of a thunderbolt
      with vinegar
when a dead hobnail
catches the course of a star
      in a bird-trap.

In the air a black plastic bag
turns to a grain of rye.
      The bark of a roasting spit
and the stump of a piece of cloth
find a worn-out fart
      and cut off its ear.

Guff is managing a fresh team of beer.

Two words are making love in a dark lane
like they never did before.
The moon opens its eyes and smiles
at the sound of distant thunder.

Guff hears it too, on the edge of elsewhere slumber.

Never again

If Guff knew what he is, he'd never
again sit on the fence
or admire some bollocks trying to be clever.

More likely, he'd jump off a cliff
or crack into pieces, laughing
at lost opportunities to cause offence.
Thank God for this kind of ignorance,

the puzzled source of the bloodmad dance.

strange courage

So up rose Guff out of sleeplessness
        flopped in the chair
                turned on the radio
                        tripped round the world
at three four five six o'clock.
The pitiless darkness began to retreat.
He listened to voices of women and men
he'd never met, would never meet,
yet felt they were friends,
friends of the night
and the drift towards morning,
voices speaking their different languages,
                words
Guff would never know how to say,
words, nevertheless,
that gave him strange courage to face
                another day.

149

Waking

Guff stretches his body with awaking questions.
Who put words on earthquakes?
Who names the stray dog?
Who remembers Lynn Klieskey's unhanged neck?
How many secrets are buried in Graffa bog?
Questions are waking up
like wild flowers growing
in a garden of no knowing.
Old mongrel Guff frisks like a terrier pup.

Around five o'clock

A grey jetline from one end of the sky to the other.
A confident half-moon in March sunlight.
Harvey's ducks enjoying canal water.
How does it feel, wonders Guff, to have
                   a sister or brother?

getting on

A writer may get on well, even very well,
with other people. He rarely gets on well
with himself.

He told himself

The dreams hammered Guff's head like stones.
Waking, he saw the sky, cosmic grave of skeletons.

Guff rocked in his chair, saying
                    over and over
'I don't give a damn,
                    I don't give a damn'
                              and then.
                    over and over,
'I am what I am,
                    I am what I am.'
          He rocked and rocked and rocked
                    all night long
the shadows in his mind danced
          to music of right and wrong
                    all night long
          and he didn't give a damn
          no he didn't give a damn

so he told himself anyway
          he told himself anyway

sadness and sodium

Guff wakes up crying, crying,
thinking, this is not my fault,
ever since my teenage years
I've had to get rid of salt.

Oldest friend

I'm the first to admit I cannot understand
why I am empty now, so empty
I could sit here all night

and wait
like a pit
to be filled with weeds and stones.

And yet without this emptiness
I wouldn't venture out
to taste the drugged city's mania and stress

or my old friends the pigeons beaking
for bread in the shadows of cobbles
where tired feet go slouching

dragging years like chains behind them
What is this emptiness and why
do I respect the bleak authority?

To live in emptiness is to wait.
To wait is to live on a stage made of nothing.
To live on a stage is to be an audience

witnessing selves play a game of chess
going on and on until I know
the hot illusion of success,

the pure dignity of failure.
Guff rises, goes to the window,
a girl with perfect buttocks lies there

on her belly reading a vast novel
which from Guff's height seems
an epic tale of good and evil,

epic enough to fill his emptiness
for an hour. She stretches her legs,
shuts novel, heads for another place.

Guff swallows her, buttocks and all.
How long is it since
he was a cannibal?

He swallows the wall, trees, grass
she has left behind.
He devours her body. Then he chews her mind.

Still he's not satisfied.
Is the world made of emptiness?
Does the earth chew billions of dead?

Are emptiness and appetite the same thing?
Is everyone eating everyone else?
Call it a state of rest, feel the earth's pulse

throbbing music for the night
advancing across fields, down roads
that are a map of appetite.

Guff turns, walks, sits, hears cries
dropping like crumbs
into his rich, abysmal emptiness.
The oldest friend he has.

One step at a time

One step at a time, hell to earth to heaven,
Tiger Woods holes from a hundred yards.
Watch out for crosswinds on the N Eleven
Weekenders shoot thousands of birds.

We move on now to that assassination
late last night in Belgrade.
A large section of the army has been called out
to deal with a Stoneybatter grenade.

What is the best value for money?
In Dublin, Cork Street is at a standstill.
The thing is to move quickly through the system
and don't forget to take your pill.

Ireland is one of the dirtiest countries in Europe
Limerick faces another housing crisis
We have a few murders every week now
Apollo should handcuff Dionysus.

Not the star

When in doubt contact your broker
Lover is fatally stabbed in bed
Negotiations look set to continue for days
A medium-to-well steak means little or no blood.

A gift for quotation doesn't mean you can think
If you don't give your name they won't know who you are
The deep thrill happens when you go to the brink
Even then, it's the starlight you see, not the star.

learning, listening

Guff doesn't complain.
He has learned
to live with his pain
listening
to the kamikaze rain
committing suicide
against the window pane.

Let

So let the well-planned phrases stab the heart
and let her feel the truth is hers alone.
Auschwitz in Dublin? How could that be art?
God help her when the hurt claims every bone
that Daddy planned, a fascist skeleton
in Wicklow heather, not far from Dublin.

Test

The sound rang through the universe
like a Christchurch bell through Dublin
but do I dare to hear it now,
Guff asks himself, as he tries
to cross a street
and reach the other side
alive.

Going to the moon
is safe enough
but crossing a Dublin street
tests every resource I have.

becoming

Surrender, first, then let your mind run free
back to the moment when the hurt began
and the first thrust of ecstasy
saw a trembling boy become a trembling man.

could be

every word Guff hears
could be the first word
ever uttered, so as years
try to wither his eyes
and ears, he struggles
to taste what once he
tasted with boyish joy:
surprise.

At Mass

(from the Irish)

Light of my soul, how lightly you move
Towards the gift of the only God of love.
I approach the Host to share God's body and blood,
I look at you and my soul begins to shred.

The Faces

To face the faces stabbing his life
A man should be a smiling knife.

Style

When she said 'I love you, I love you'
Guff didn't know what to say,
he turned away

and looked at the canal
where a duck was impressing another duck
with a frisky duckstyle.

Does Guff have style?
Is this whole man (whole?)
expanded, imprinted, made recognisable

in expression? Is he compounded
of consciousness and unconsciousness,
spontaneity and effort

with, now and then,
a smidgin of calculation
tossed in?

Has he a way of saying himself,
regardless of what he says
so that the hypnotist is hypnotised?

Does he possess that daring negligence,
mesmeric indifference,
sheer careless magnificence

of sound and gesture
which God may give to ducks
but deny to men?

If Guff said 'quack'
would she still say 'I love you'?
He's going, going, he's not looking back,

he may trace this canal to its source
in flat fields by dark hills.
He's on the run from style,

from a moment of knowing
and the poor devil will never say
which way the wind is blowing.

Well, not until he learns from creatures on the wing
so that whatever sound he makes
makes people say 'Good Lord! Guff can sing'.

Laurel

(from the Greek of Achilles Paraschos)

Do not envy me, do not
envy the laurel-tree.
You water my roots with blood

and burning tears. He's a lucky man
who never seeks laurels
but settles for roses.

I am the crown
of glory and pain, friend
of the battered outcasts of fortune.

Sick envy poisons my leaves.
That is the reason I crown
the poets of the world.